Do you remember?

THE BOOK THAT TAKES YOU BACK

BY
MICHAEL GITTER
AND
SYLVIE ANAPOL

GIFT BOOKS from Hallmark

CHRONICLE BOOKS
SAN FRANCISCO

DESIGN & ART DIRECTION:
Red Herring Design
Carol Bobolts
Kayt de Fever
Deb Schuler

PHOTOGRAPHY:
Archive Photos, The Bettmann Archive, Black Star/Stern,
The Milton H. Greene Archives, Photofest New York, H. Armstrong Roberts,
Schultz/Sunshine/Retna Ltd., Joe Steinmetz, Superstock Inc., Joe Wittkop

FLAP AND COVER COPY: Suzanne Falter-Barns

MANY THANKS TO:
Karen Alters, Peter Clemens, Patricia Eisemann, Rick Gell, Cindy Gitter, Erika Glazer, Deena Greenberg, Caroline Herter, Emily Miller, Caryn Nathanson, Robert Tucker, Paul Vaccari, our families, staff, friends and contributors around the country, and most especially Dick & Dorothy Bobolts, Anna Mae and Leona Boboltz, Darcy & Sean Fernald, Art & Mary Ann Knechtel, and Christine Grove for not being afraid to search the dark recesses of their closets and garages.

This edition published in 2002 by Chronicle Books LLC exclusively for Hallmark Cards, Inc.

www.hallmark.com

ISBN 0-8118-3631-2

Manufactured in China

10 9 8 7 6 5 4 3 2

To E, Z & A

Hub-i, Frub-iends!

(Or, for those of the post–Ub era — Hi, friends!)

This book began as a few simple reminiscences on a Saturday drive. The question at the time was Mystery Date—specifically, who was the preferred date, which somehow led us onto edible Creepy Crawlers and who sent away for the Muscular Dystrophy Carnival Kit. A good hour or so later a parlor game had been born, and it hasn't stopped yet. Since then, we've noticed a few things.

Once the question "Do you remember?" comes up, it is literally impossible to keep from reminiscing. It's almost as if you *have* to sit there and debate whether any of The Monkees could actually play the guitar.

Secondly, it appears there are certain experiences common to all American childhoods:

- the irresistible urge to unroll a Yodel
- small green turtles that lived in a plastic dish with a fake plastic palm tree on an island in the middle (note: the turtles always died)
- the smell of mimeograph paper
- losing Lite-Brite pegs in the shag carpet
- getting to stay up late on Friday nights to watch *Love, American Style*

Whether you put jimmies or sprinkles on your ice cream, the cultural experience of growing up in this country was essentially the same. This book is an historic work that celebrates some of the innocence, the sweetness, and the common connections of a time gone by.

Without further ado, it's sock it to me time.

Michael and Sylvie

P.S. The pages here are organized randomly, like memories often are. If you want to see whether we've included your own particular favorites, though, check the index in the back. If it's not there, send it to the Do You Remember? Company for Volume Two.

MIA bracelets the women's

ERA Hanoi Hilton 1A status

draft dodgers burn the bra Huntley

streakers transcendental

Love Canal casualty reports on the evening news

Governor George Wallace

movement Gasohol Anita Bryant

leaded gasoline

& Brinkley the sound of the Teletype

meditation Walter Cronkite

"I am not a crook"

Aleksandr Solzhenitsyn The PLO

BEFORE
CABLE
TELE
VISION

Gomer Pyle
Green Acres
Lassie
My Three Sons
McHale's Navy
Gilligan's Island
This Is Your Life
Candid Camera with Allan Funt
The Ghost and Mrs. Muir
5

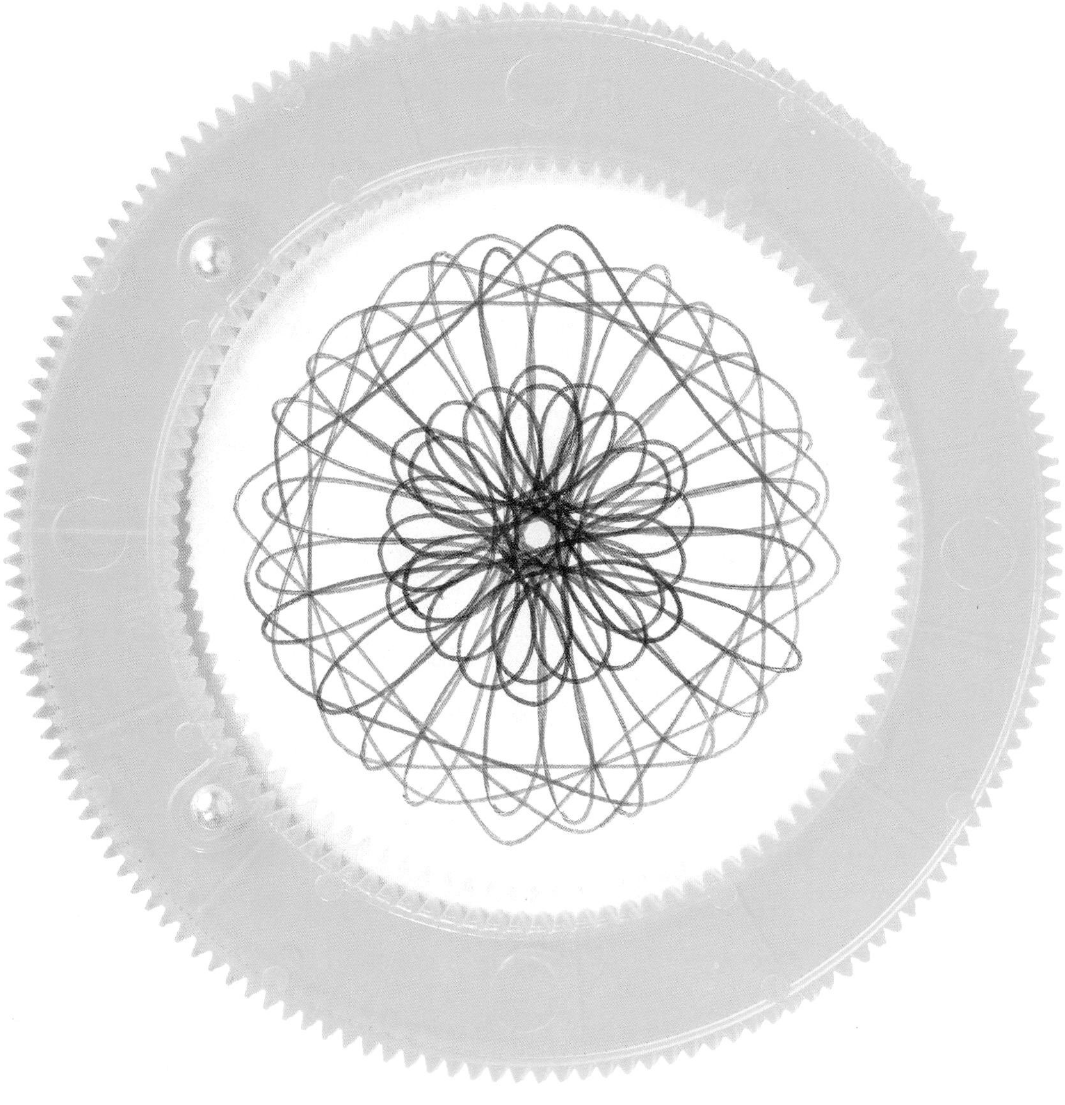

1 Keith loved his 1952 Hudson, but it kept him broke.
2 He asked his mother, Shirley, for a loan, but she said no.
3 Keith left. Chris wondered why his mom was still talking!
4 Keith didn't have any better luck with Laurie.
5 "I'll lend money," said Danny, "if you let me be your manager."
6 At dinner, Danny announced that he was Keith's money manager.
7 It was time to leave for a singing engagement.
REEL 1
A
THE PARTRIDGE FAMILY
gaf VIEW-MASTER Stereo Reel
MADE IN U.S.A.
GAF CORPORATION
New York, N.Y. U.S.A.
T.M. Reg. U.S. Pat. Off.
©1971 and Trademark of Columbia Pictures Industries, Inc. - All Rights Reserved - GAF, Authorized User.
B 5691

BEATLES: ALL 4 MARRIED?
SEPT
16
25c
MAGAZINE
PDC
ROLLING STONES
THEY GET AWAY WITH MURDER!
DAVE CLARK 5
50 INTIMATE QUESTIONS
BEACH BOYS "FEUD"
WHAT'S IT ALL ABOUT?
ELVIS out? PETERSEN in?
WRITE A LETTER TO
PAUL ★ GEORGE
RINGO ★ JOHN
& GET A PERSONAL ANSWER
WIN 50 FAB
BEATLE
NECK-CHAINS!
LANDON VS.
PERNELL
SCOOP ON THE BIG
BONANZA BREAK-UP
IT'S
GEAR,
DEAR!
THRILLING TRUE STORY
A GIRL'S 3 DAYS
WITH THE
BEATLES!
PIMPLES
BLACKHEADS
ACNE
HOW TO GET RID
OF THEM
BEATLE'S HOME ADDRESSES

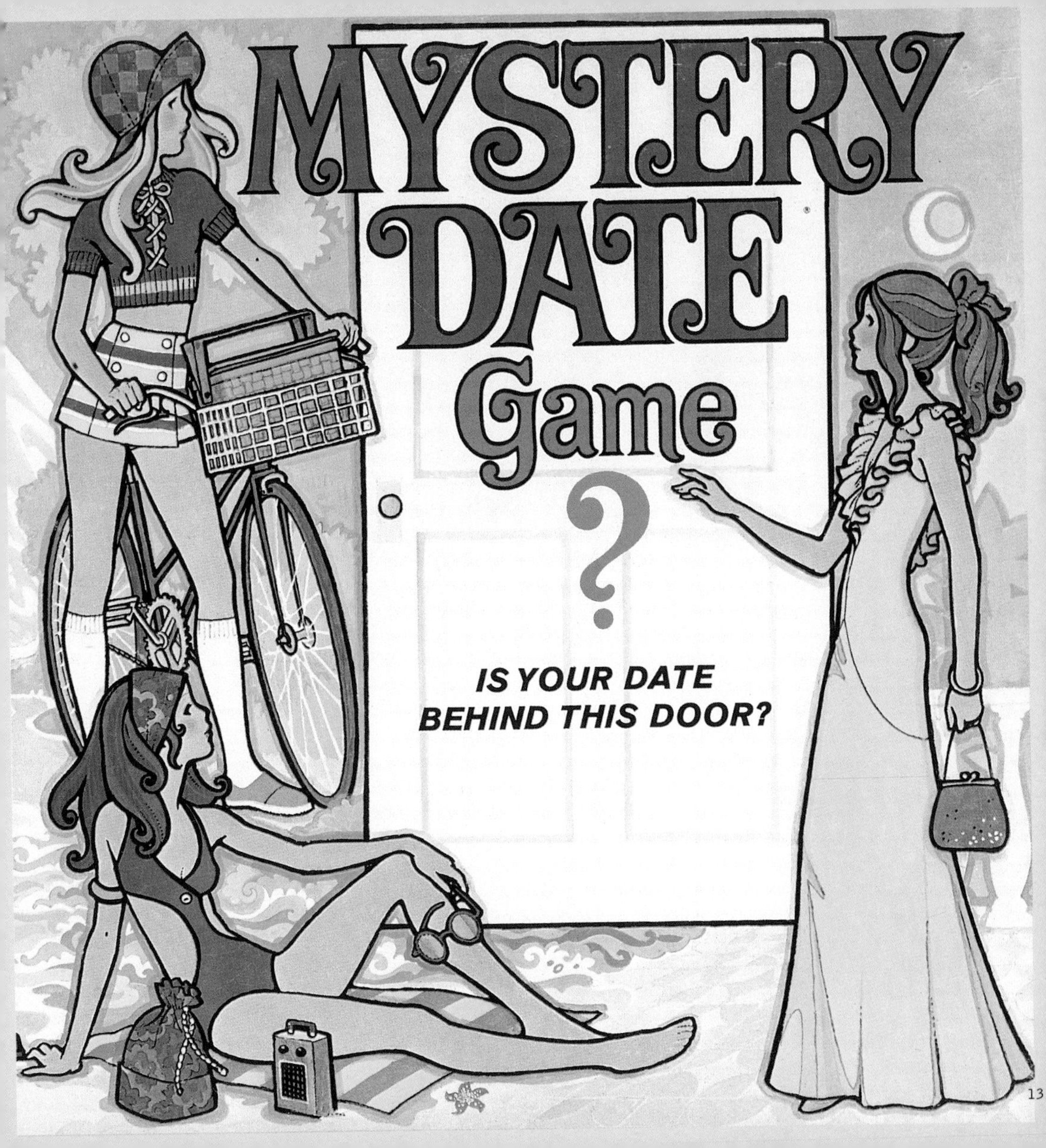
MYSTERY DATE Game
?
IS YOUR DATE
BEHIND THIS DOOR?

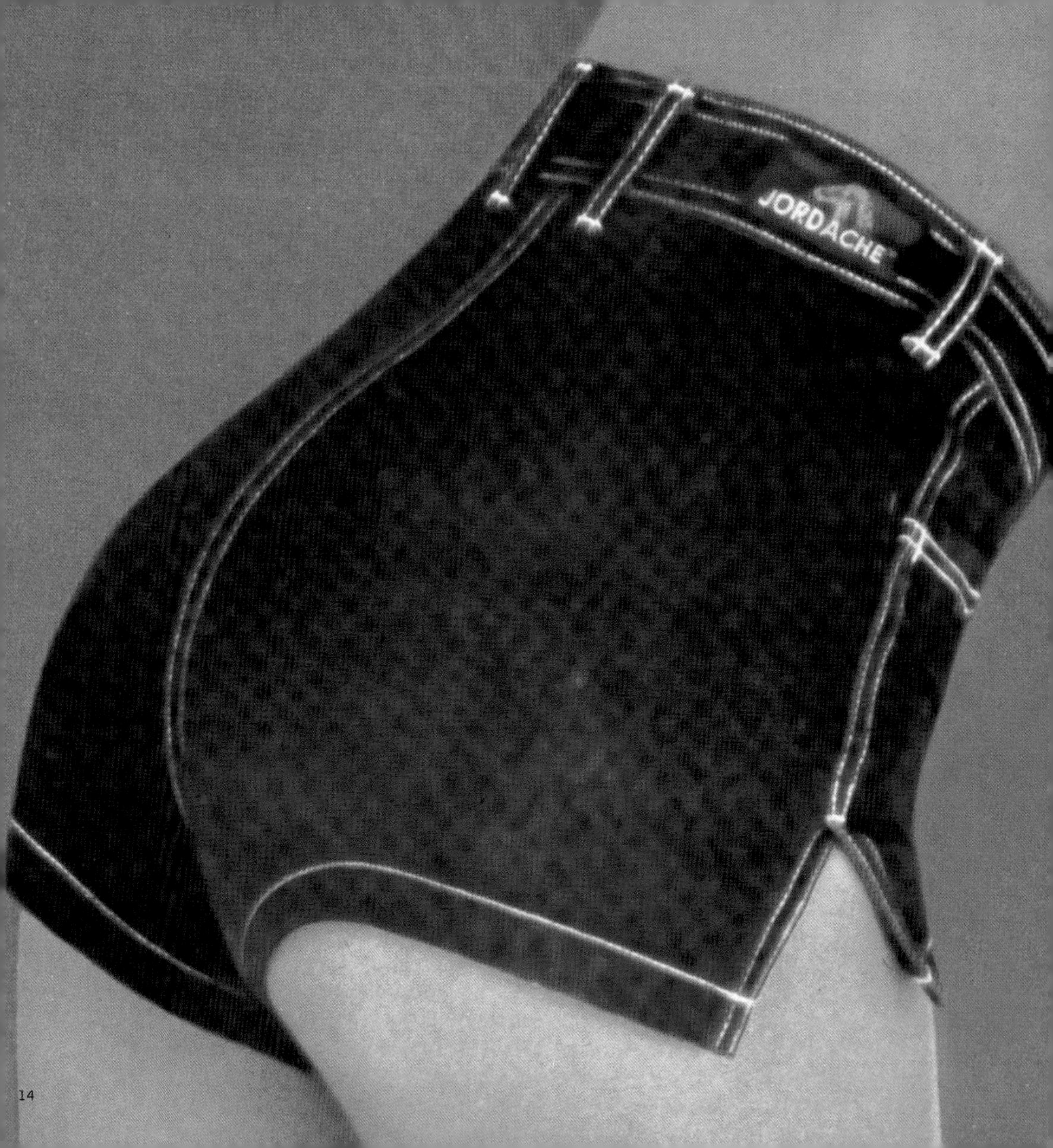
JORDACHE

Sergio Valente Gloria Vanderbilt

"Nothing comes between me and my Calvins"

Sasson Knickers Levi's Bend Overs

bellbottoms bleach-blotched jeans

culottes tube tops bib overalls

Gunne Sax dresses Aigner basket purses

pantsuits gauchos minis, midis & maxis

ponchos halters Halston Izod Wranglers

Ten-O-Six
Clearasil
green lipstick
Ipana toothpaste
Mr. Bubble
CanoeCanoe
Toni home perms
Vitalis
Hai Karate cologne
Stridex Pads
Phisodex
Photo Unavailable
Kissing Potion
Avon Skin-So-Soft
Halston Z-17
Blue frosted eyeshadow

Hires
LIP SMACKER
BIT-O-HONEY
LIP SMACKER by BONNE BELL
Tootsie Roll
LIP-SMACKER
GOOD and PLENTY
BONNE BELL
Sour Grapes
7up
The Uncola
LIP
Lipton
ORANGE
Crush
LIP SMACKER
Dr Pepper
LIP SMACKER
STRAWBERRY
SMACKER
RASPBERRY

Afro picks
Shags
Beehives
Alberto VO5
Feathered hair
Teased hair
Short N' Sassy
Long & Silky
Wigs
Ducktails
Breck Shampoo
Clairol Herbal

Photo: © 1966 [illegible] H. Greene

"I told two friends and they told two friends and so on, and so on..."

"Gee, Your Hair Smells Terrific!"

Johnson & Johnson's No More Tears formula

"Which twin has the Toni?"

"Only your hairdresser knows for sure."

Lemon-up

Love's Baby Soft Shampoo

VCRs COSTING $1,000

CALLING AN OPERATOR TO DIAL LONG DISTANCE UHF

DITTOS BETAMAX

HANDHELD BATTERY-OPERATED FANS CPM

BEFORE 911 WHEN ONLY DOCTORS HAD BEEPERS

BEING AFRAID OF MICROWAVES

TRANSISTOR RADIOS APPLE LISA COMPUTERS

LIFE BEFORE ATMS LIFE BEFORE ANSWERING MACHINES

PANASONIC LOOP RADIOS BEFORE FAXES

ONE PHONE COMPANY TURNTABLES

LIFE BEFORE CAR PHONES OSBORNE COMPUTERS TANDYCRAFTS

Manual Typewriters

ZAPMAIL BY FEDEX IBM PC,JR.

ELEPHANT DISKETTES CARBON PAPER

KAYPRO COMPUTERS

GHI
DEF
ABC
PRS
TUV
WXY
1400

Jarts

Twenty Mule Team Borax

Swing Sets "No more dishpan hands"

Beanbag Chairs Bunk Beds

Rabbit Ear Antennas Tree Houses

Frigidaires Crock–Pots

Macramé Plant Hangers Waxing linoleum floors

Pooper–scoopers "kalaka!"

Bendix Washing Machines

Clothespins Wringers

waxy yellow buildup Venus Flytraps

Princess Phones

Newspaper Routes

Photos ©1966 Joe Steinmetz

SPERRY AND HUTCHINSON
S&H
DISCOUNT FOR CASH

Safari fold-up bicycles

Raleigh bicycles

streamers

Big Wheels

Columbia bicycles

3-speeds

handlebar bells

generator lights

tricycles

Chopper bicycles

banana seats

Schwinn

Huffy

baseball cards in spokes

NEW
U.S.A. MADE
Wooly Willy
TM
INSTRUCTIONS ON BACK
"MAGNETIC PERSONALITY"
DRAW WHISKERS, HAIR, AND EYEBROWS
WITH THIS MAGIC WAND
AGES 4+
WOOLY WILLY
Model No. 32N
MCMXCII
SMETHPORT SPECIALTY CO. SMETHPORT, PA 16749

chinese checkers

gyroscope

mexican jumping beans

slingshots

paper fortune tellers

kazoos

colorforms

hopscotch

shaker-makers

super elastic bubble plastic

rock polishing machines

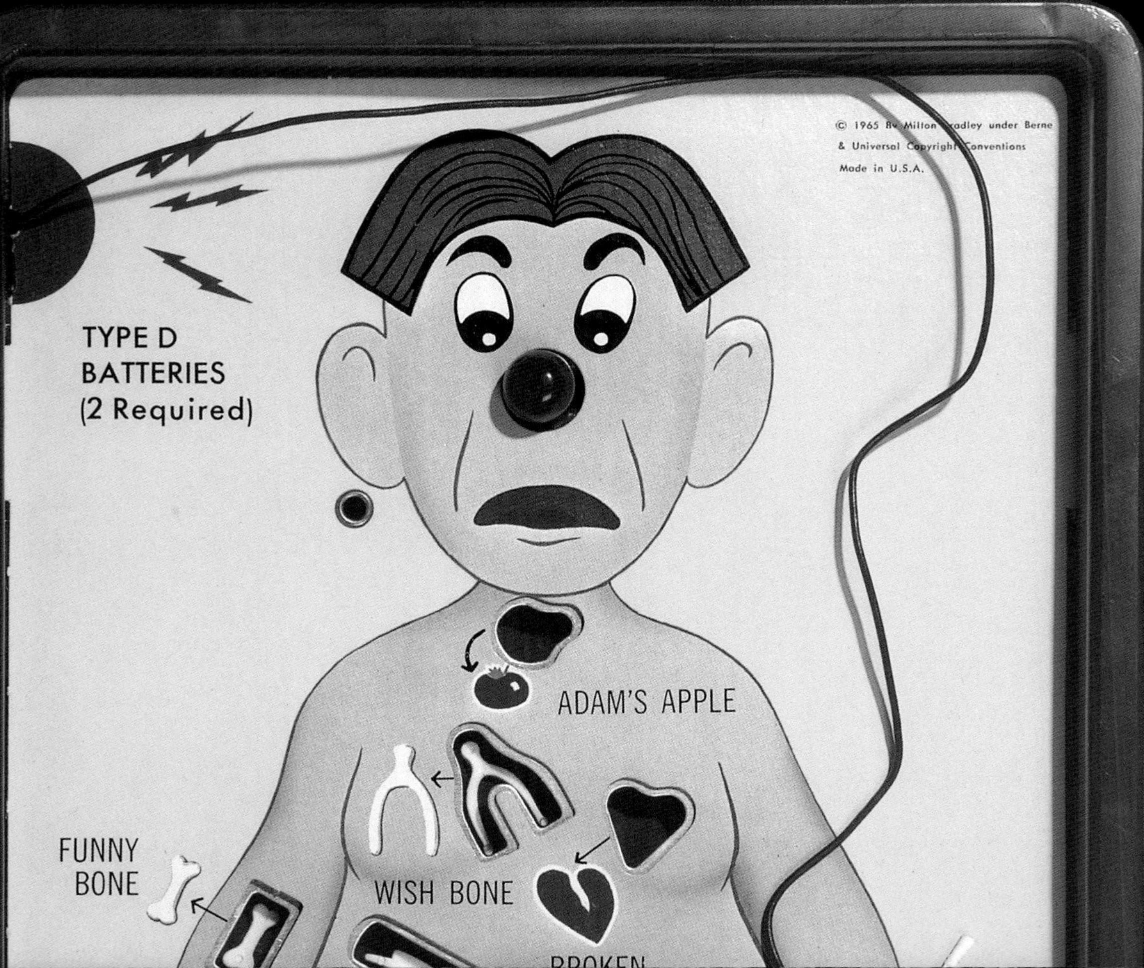

© 1965 By Milton Bradley under Berne
& Universal Copyright Conventions
Made in U.S.A.
TYPE D
BATTERIES
(2 Required)
ADAM'S APPLE
FUNNY
BONE
WISH BONE

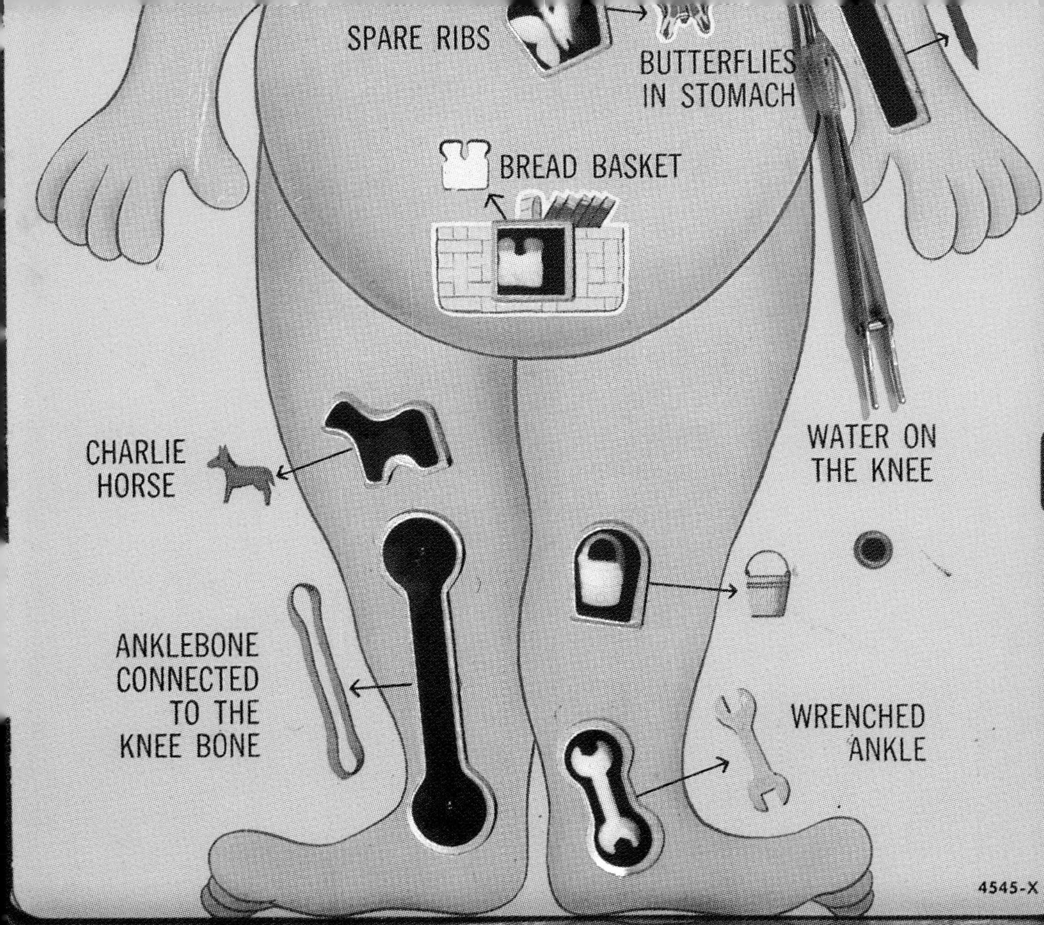

SPARE RIBS
BUTTERFLIES IN STOMACH
BREAD BASKET
CHARLIE HORSE
WATER ON THE KNEE
ANKLEBONE CONNECTED TO THE KNEE BONE
WRENCHED ANKLE
4545-X

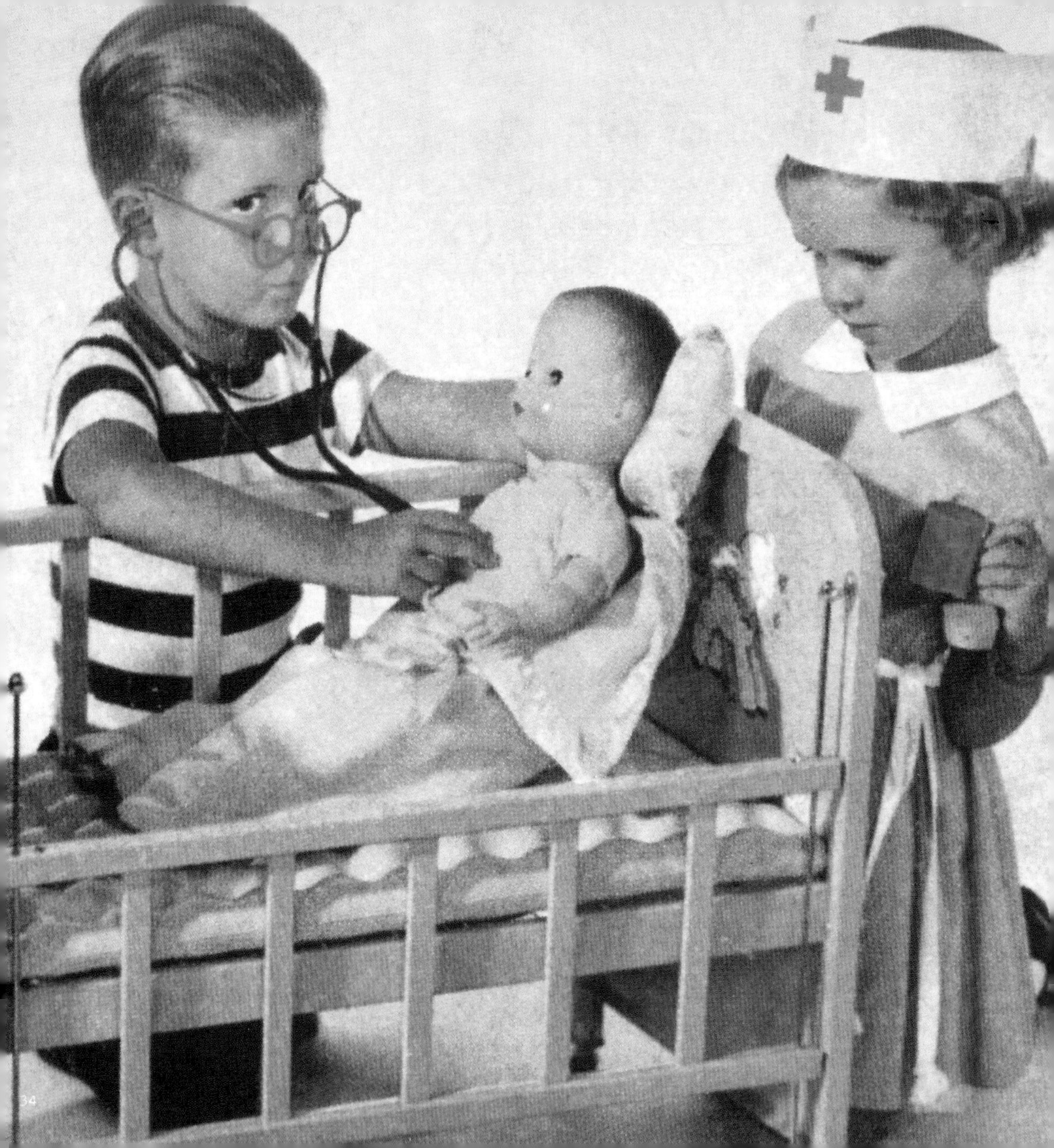

G

YOUR FIRST KISS

PG

SPIN THE BOTTLE

R

SEVEN MINUTES IN HEAVEN

X

DEEP THROAT

balconies

Saturday matinees

cartoons before the feature

drive-ins

seeing your first R movie

before multiplexes

the machine that would drop the cup
after the beverage started to pour

ushers

smoking in theaters

6

PARAMOUNT PICTURES presents
A DINO DE LAURENTIIS PRODUCTION
JANE FONDA
SEE
BARBARELLA
DO HER THING!

Bye Bye Birdie Planet of the Apes
Jaws
hat Darn Cat! Flubber Godzilla
Fame Bob & Carol & Ted & Alice
Taxi Driver
The Parent Trap Goldfinger
Goodbye, Mr. Chips
The Graduate Mary Poppins
Star Wars
Easy Rider The Incredible Mr. Limpet
A Funny Thing Happened on the Way to the Forum The Exorcist
Herbie the Love Bug
Love Story Valley of the Dolls
Where Angels Go Trouble Follows
Catch-22 M*A*S*H* The Godfather
Quadrophenia To Sir With Love
The Computer Wore Tennis Shoes
Lady and the Tramp 101 Dalmatians
Chitty Chitty Bang Bang
Willy Wonka & the Chocolate Factory

daisy chains

headbands

lava lamps

beaded curtains

god's eyes

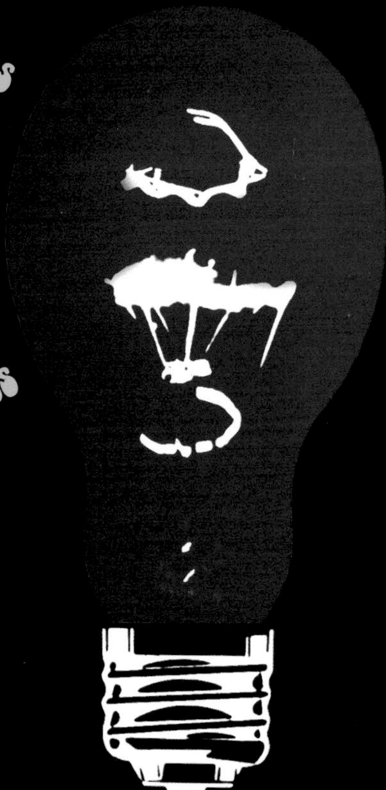

BILL GRAHAM PRESENTS IN SAN FRANCISCO
TUES. WED. THURS. ONLY
FRI. SAT. SUN. ONLY
THE DOORS
PLUS ALL WEEK
JAMES COTTON BLUES BAND
RICHIE HAVENS
FILLMORE

MARY
HOPKIN
T R O
Organization
5.05
1801
X46416
HOSE
WERE
THE
DAYS
Gene Raskin
Produced by Paul McCartney

One
Billy Don't Be a Hero
Time in a Bottle
ña Colada Song

Downtown
Kung Fu Fighting
ight Chicago Died
Classical Gas

Let Me Be There
Pop Muzik
Brand New Key
Seasons in the Sun

Superstitious
Let's Stay Together
Theme from Shaft
Proud Mary

Burn Rubber (Why You Wanna Hurt Me)
ABC-123
We Are Family

Crocodile Rock
Afternoon Delight
Knock Three Times
Fernando

STAYING ALIVE

Gloria Gaynor

Studio 54

light-up dance floors

Mirror Balls

Quiana

The Pointer Sisters

The Bump

Hooked On Classics

K.C. and the Sunshine Band

Saturday Night Fever

Xanadu

Donna Summer

The Bee Gees

Roller Disco

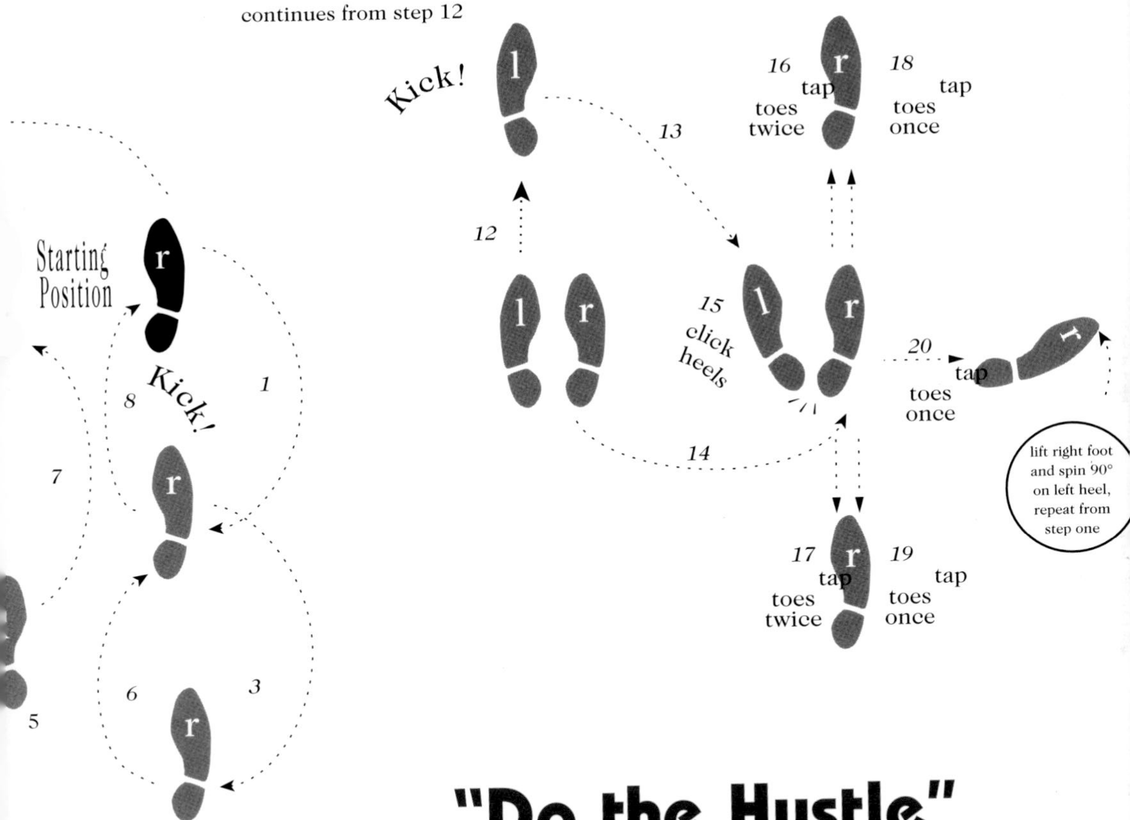

"Do the Hustle"

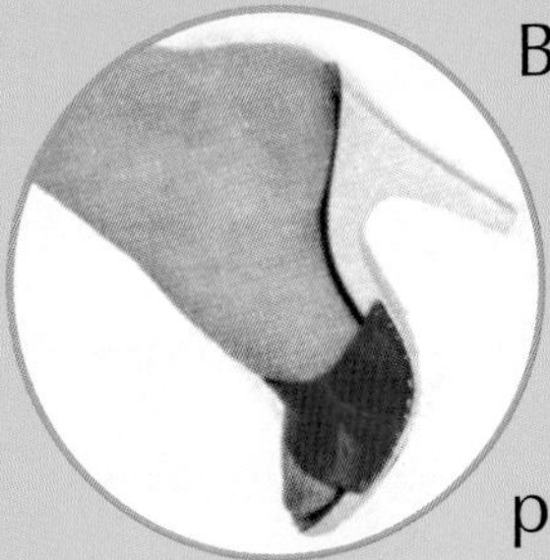

Bass Weejuns • Courreges boots

Chukka boots • Jack Purcells

Capezios • Earth Shoes • Vans

platforms • P F Flyers • Zips

saddle shoes • Mary Janes • Pumas

Converse Chuck Taylor high-tops • clogs

Adidas • Frye boots • Topsiders

Hush Puppies • Deckers • wedgies

patent leather • Bucks • Papagallos

Red Ball Jets • penny loafers

Double S sneakers •

galoshes • flip-flops

Buster Brown and his

dog Tiger • Cherokees

"Right foot yellow."

Losing Lite-Brite

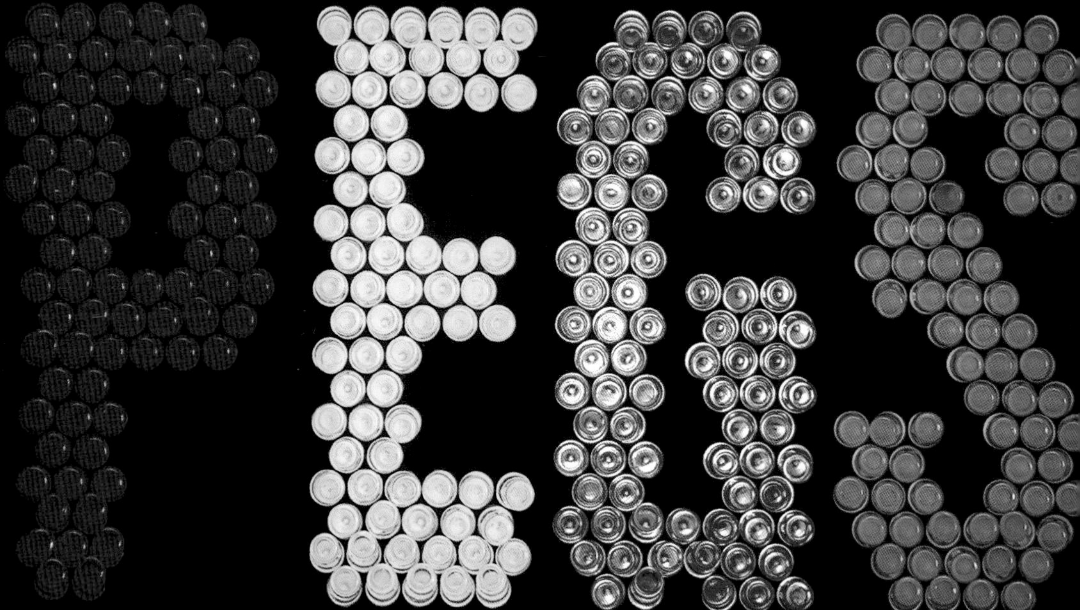

in the ·················►

Jack LaLanne on TV

USFL Olga Korbut

Jim McMahon

Dr. J Pee Wee Reese

Mickey Mantle

Henry Aaron

Leon Spinks

Lew Alcindor

Babe Ruth

The Baltimore Colts

Earl the Pearl & Wilt the Stilt

Cassius Clay

Jackie Stewart

Secretariat

Willie Mays

Ilie Nastase
Bjorn Borg
Tracy Austin
John McEnroe
Chris Evert
Billie Jean King
Bobby Riggs
Arthur Ashe
Evonne Goolagong
Franklin
3107
Hi-Point

Photo: © Terry O'Neill/Black Star/Stern

Israel's team taken hostage at the 1972 Summer Olympics in Munich • New York "Miracle Mets" • President Carter's boycott of the 1980 Summer Olympics in Russia • The "Thrilla in Manila" • American team wins Gold medal in ice hockey at 1980 Winter Olympics • Joe Namath dons pantyhose for L'eggs ad • Muhammad Ali is stripped of championship for not fighting in the Vietnam War due to religious beliefs • New York Jets win Super Bowl III (1969) to become the first AFL team to win the championship • Hank Aaron hits 715th home run to break Babe Ruth's record • George Steinbrenner fires Billy Martin—the first time • Roberto Clemente, hero of the 1970 World Series, dies in an Everglades plane crash on the way to help Nicaraguan earthquake victims • Miami Dolphins go undefeated in 1973's 14-game season and win the Super Bowl • Joe Theismann breaks his leg • Nadia Comaneci's Olympic "10"

Rubber Duckie, you're the one. You make bathtime lots of fun. Rubber Duckie, I'm awfully fond of you. **Rubber Duckie**, joy of joys, when I squeeze you, you make noise. Rubber Duckie, you're my very best friend, it's true. Every day when I make my way to the tubby, I find a little fella who's cute and yella and chubby. **Rubadub-dubby**. Rubber Duckie, you're so fine and I'm lucky that you're mine. Rubber Duckie, I'm awfully fond of you.

dinnerware from the movies

terrariums

Popeil's Pocket Fisherman

Formica dinettes

coughing ashtrays

Ginsu Knives

Seal-a-Meal

Dixie riddle cups

Gas Station Glassware and Knives

Chia Pet

kaleidoscopes

head shops

patchouli oil

Incense

black velvet paintings

batik

Nehru jackets

Woodstock Beatniks Cheech And Chong Fringe Vests SDS Gray Panthers Flower Power

Central Park Be-Ins

Haight Ashbury

LYDIA

Kewpie dolls
Stretch Armstrong
Betsy Wetsy
G.I. Joe with Kung Fu grip
Mrs. Beasley
Malibu Barbie

Charlie's Angels dolls
Chrissie
Dressy Bessy & Dapper Dan
Holly Hobbie
Flatsy
Liddle Kiddles

string art • clay handprints • decoupage •

• woodburning sets • Heathkits

model kits • finger painting •

stamp collecting • finger knitting

• airplane glue

ght sets, with sensa-
ntrol for uncoupling
eel drive locomotive!

"Manumatic" Control—one of the new 1948 Lionel features, found only in the colorful "Scout" line! Cars uncouple going forward or in reverse at the pressure of the "Manumatic" button. Track section to which control unit is affixed can be placed anywhere on layout.

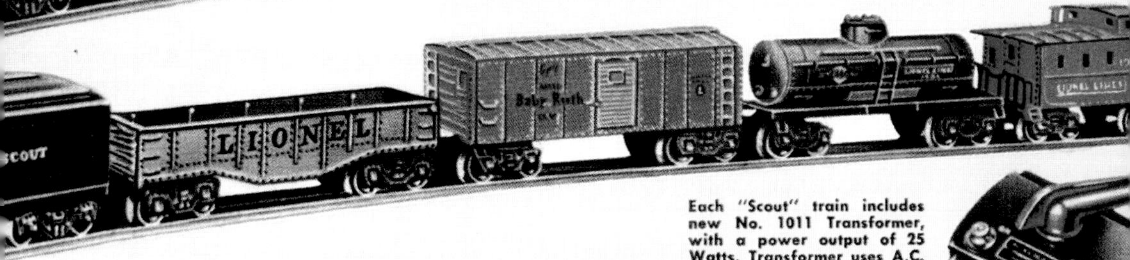

Each "Scout" train includes new No. 1011 Transformer, with a power output of 25 Watts. Transformer uses A.C. current only.

T

t. Cars have
"Manumatic"
reverses by
n set is 41½

—1 No. 1002
s No. 1013

1595

HT

colored cars
with realistic
. Locomotive
Extraordinary
½" x 27⅜".
nder—1 No.
7 Caboose—

No. 1656LT "027" AND "O" GAUGE S

With Built-in AUTOMATIC BELL

This powerful, realistic Switcher Locomotive and Tender may b
separately. A perfectly-proportioned model of the "yard goats"

The Little Engine That Could
Petticoat Junction
Trainfares lower than airfares
Murder On the Orient Express
Soul Train
Silver Streak
"Choo-Choo Charlie
was an engineer . . ."

L I

F E

B E F

O R E

F E D

E X

TEXACO
OFFICIAL
ATE OF NEW YORK
OTOR VEHICLE
PECTION STATION
BRAKE
Special
4 WHEELS
RELINED
99 9
Gas
Sales Tax
Total
INCLUDES ALL TAXES
TOTAL SALE
GALLONS
87
LEADED
No OPEN No
GAS FOR GAS
SERVICE
AND
REPAIRS
ONLY

THE PACER

Yugos **El Camino**

DeLorean

Baby-on-Board signs **Maverick**

LEVI'S EDITION GREMLIN

"What's your handle?" **leaded gasoline**

DODGE DUSTER

Subaru Brat

"Are we

there yet?"

Pinto

Datsun 280Z GASOHOL

AMC HORNET

dogs with bouncing heads

"10-4 Good Buddy"

VOLKSWAGEN THING

mopeds **VW Beetle**

THE RAMBLER **Chevy Luv**

simon • don't break the ice • ants-in-your-pants • cootie • kerplunk • hand
chutes and ladders • slime • wish-niks • vampire blood • silly putty

down • gnip gnop • hungry hungry hippo • wizzers
squirmels • trouble • mousetrap • magnetic football

c k s

the osmond brothers

the starland vocal band

tony orlando and dawn

the captain and tennille

peter lemongello

joey travolta

the hues corporation

olivia newton-john

tiny tim

kristy & jimmy mcnichol

elton john & kiki dee

the carpenters

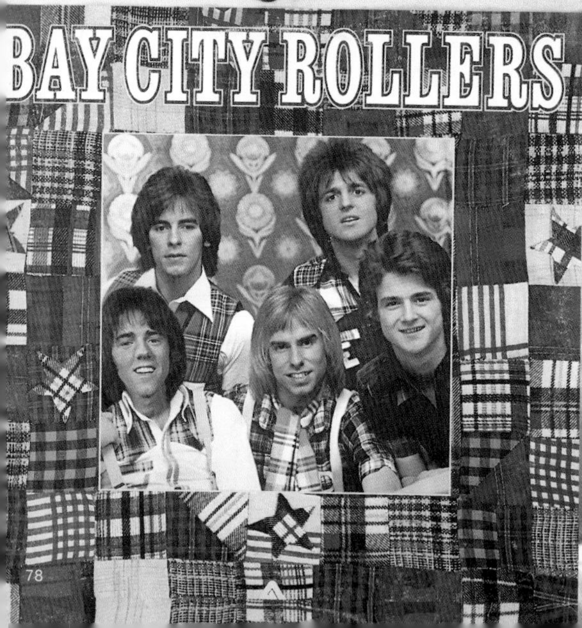

EIF GARRETT
Feel the Need

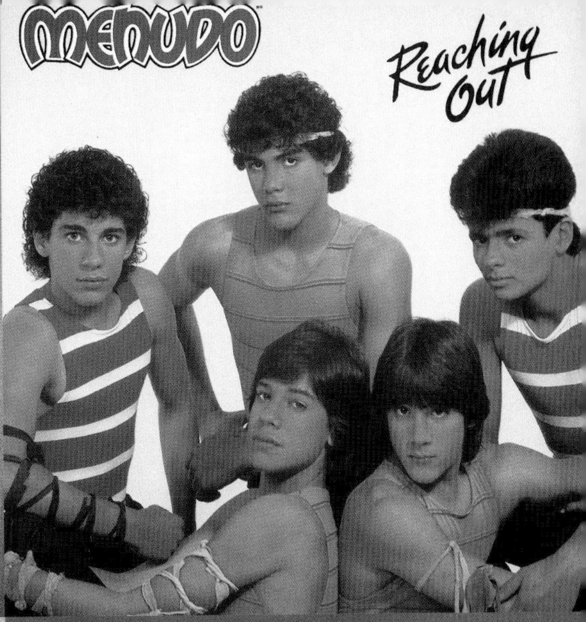
MENUDO
Reaching Out

THE DeFRANCO FAMILY FEATURING TONY DeFRANCO
SAVE THE LAST DANCE FOR ME
"SAVE THE LAST DANCE FOR ME" "LOVE THE WAY YOU DO" "THE ONLY ONE" "BECAUSE WE BOTH ARE YOUNG" "WRITE ME A LETTER"
"HOLD ME" "I GUESS YOU ALREADY KNEW" "POOR BOY" "BABY BLUE" "MAYBE IT'S YOU"
RECORDS

STEREO
DIANA ROSS
presents
THE JACKSON 5
I WANT YOU BACK
ZIP A DEE DOO DAH • NOBODY
CAN YOU REMEMBER
STANDING IN THE SHADOWS OF LOVE
YOU'VE CHANGED • MY CHERIE AMOUR
WHO'S LOVING YOU
(I KNOW) I'M LOSING YOU • CHAINED
STAND • BORN TO LOVE YOU
MS-129V1

"I'm a little bit country…"

"… and I'm a little bit rock 'n' roll"

Charlie's Angels

The Man from Atlantis Welcome Back, Kotter

Mork and Mindy Beat the Clock

Let's Make a Deal Emergency!

The Gong Show

Baretta Don Kirshner's Rock Concert

The White Shadow Lou Grant

Three's Company Soap

The Tomorrow Show Adam-12

CHiPS Columbo

The Love Boat

Fantasy Island

Fernwood 2-Night

Truth or Consequences

"a three-hour tour" KOJAK

THE MIKE DOUGLAS SHOW The Dating Game

SIX MILLION DOLLAR MAN

ZOOM HOGAN'S HEROES

GRAMMAROCK

LAND OF THE LOST

THE BIONIC WOMAN

HAPPY DAYS

IT'S MY WORLD AND WELCOME TO IT

"PORK CHOPS AND APPLESAUCE"

DYNOMITE! JAMES AT 16

"DANGER! DANGER! WILL ROBINSON" Match Game '74

PLEASE DON'T LITTER
DISPOSE OF PROPERLY

Twoallbeefpattiesspecialsaucelettuce

eesepicklesonionsonasesameseedbun.

CHARLIE

"I'd like to buy the world a Coke."

"It's Shake 'N Bake and I helped."

"Nobody doesn't like Sara Lee."

"I'd *walk a mile* for a Camel."

"I'd rather fight than switch."

"Ruffles have r-r-r-idges."

"Ho, Ho, Ho, Green Giant."

"Winston tastes good like a cigarette should."

"Plop Plop, Fizz Fizz, oh what a relief it is!"

"Ask any mermaid you happen to see . . ."

When it says Libby's, Libby's, Libby's on the label, label, label, you will like it, like it, like it on your table, table, table.

Oh Oh, Spaghettios!

BATTLESTAR
GALACTICA
TM

Take away 1.

How many? 6

How many left? ____

Take away 1.

How many? 5

How many left? ____

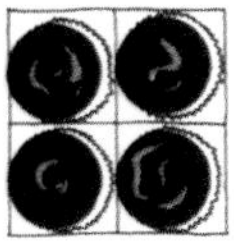

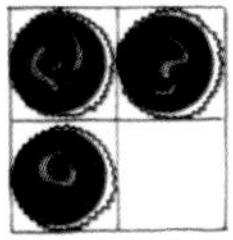

Take away 1.

How many? ____

How many left? ____

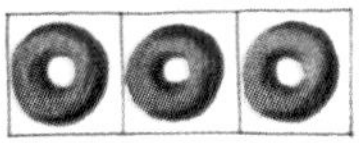

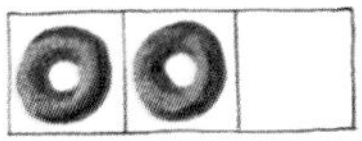

Take away 1.

How many? ____

How many left? ____

Take away 1.

How many? ____

How many left? ____

Your First Grade Teacher

book reports

lunch money

kickball

bread and butter in waxed paper bags

the kid who ate paste

number two pencils

hall monitors

tetherball

little cartons of milk and graham crackers

spitballs

permission slips

decorating lunch boxes

book covers

box of 64 Crayolas with sharpener

protractors

I pledge allegiance to the
flag of the United States
of America, and to the
Republic for which it
stands, one nation under
God, indivisible, with
liberty and justice for all.

Dick said, “Hello, Tom.
Hello, Susan.
Stop and play with Jane and me.”

“Please do,” said Jane.
“Come in and see our house.
I am the mother.
Dick is the father.
Sally is the baby.”

Goodnight Moon Boys' Life
Highlights
Gulliver's Travels
Madeline
Treasur
The Lord of the Rings The Five Chinese Brothers

Weekly
Dr. Doolittle
Curious George Charlotte's Web
The Cat in
Where the Wild Things Are
Pat the Bunny
Peter
The Bobbsey Twins

A Wrinkle in Time

Misty

Ranger Rick

The Giving Tree

Island

Little House on the Prairie

Babar

Eloise

Reader

Trixie Belden

Harriet the Spy

Judy Blume

the Hat

Winnie-the-Pooh

The Swiss Family Robinson

Pan

Black Beauty

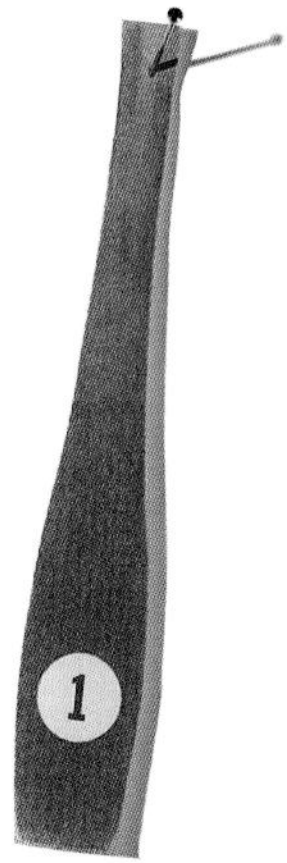

HOLIDAY PAGEANTS

GOING TO BIRTHDAY PARTIES

LEAVING MILK AND COOKIES FOR SANTA

PLAYING DREIDEL

EXCHANGING VALENTINES

MAKING HAND TURKEYS

THE TOOTH FAIRY

THE LAST DAY OF SCHOOL BEFORE SUMMER

HANUKKAH GELT

TRICK-OR-TREATING

THE EASTER BUNNY

MUSCULAR DYSTROPHY CARNIVAL KITS

On my Honor, I will try:
To do my duty to God and my country,
To help other people at all times,
And to obey the Girl Scout Law.

Webelos
Synchronized Swimmers
Slumber Parties
Boy Scouts
Brownies
Red Plaque-detecting Tablets
Lemonade Stands
Playing Dress-up
Going to the Circus
Little League

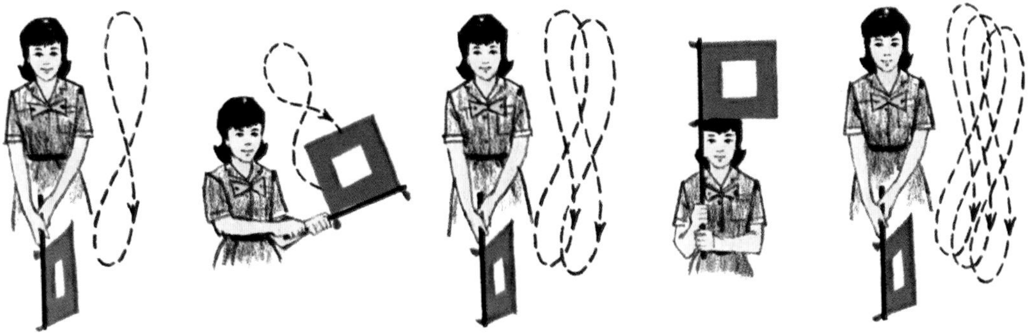

The World's Fair
Standing on a Swing
Retainers & Head Gear
The Mumps
Piano Lessons
Crank Calls
Ballet Class
Recitals
Ig-pay atin-lay

BAR OO
BAR OO

HOW TO MAKE S'MORES

You'll need: 2 graham crackers, 1/3 of a 1 1/2-ounce bar of milk chocolate, and 1 marshmallow

1. Toast marshmallow to a golden brown

2. Put it in a sandwich with the chocolate between two crackers

3. Press together gently and eat

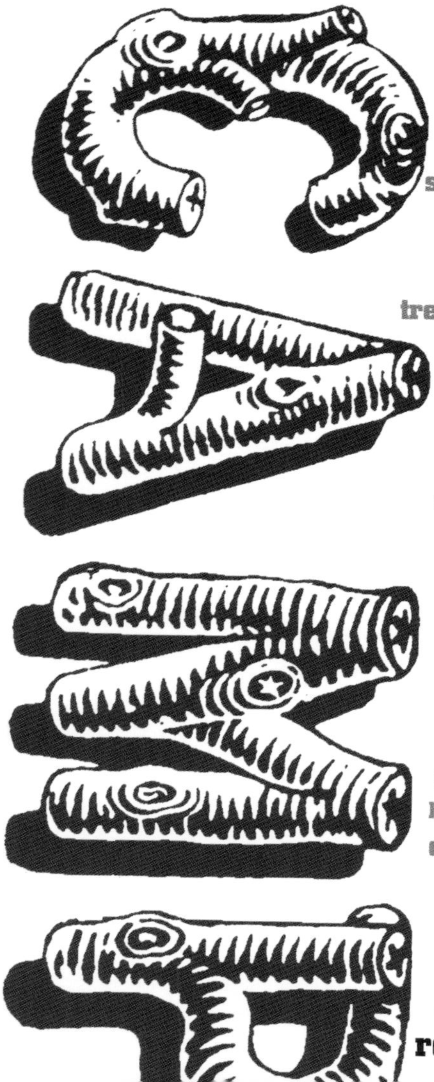

reveille
hospital corners
smoking behind the bunk
nametags in clothes
bats in the social hall
Sexton institutional food
treasure hunts
bunk beds
outstanding camper award
lights out
color war
archery
mess hall
canoes
collapsible water cups
care packages
canteen
t u g - o f - w a r
pre-addressed postcards
hiking
cookouts
being homesick
tents
telephone calls from home
softball
root beer barrels

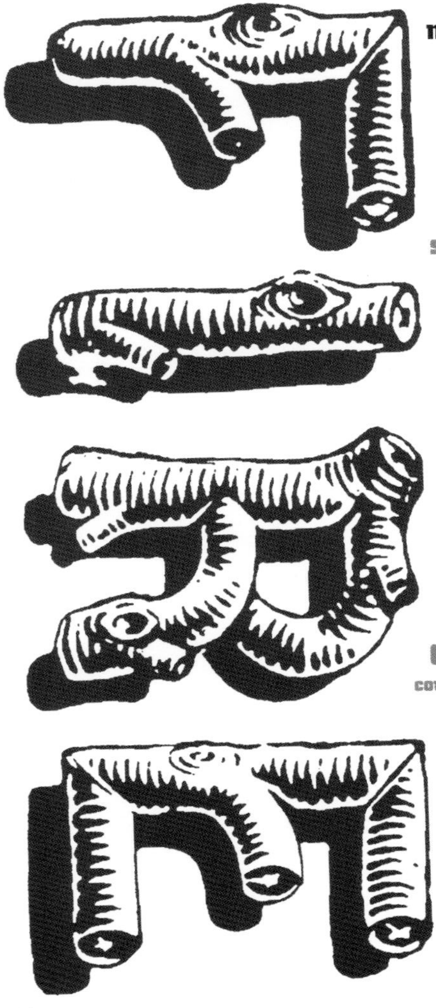

flashlights
uniforms
mosquitoes
ghost stories
CIT's
arts & crafts
lanyard
shadow puppets
raids
sing-alongs
parents' day
water-skiing
pillow fights
muddy lake
cropsy maniac
medicine line at the infirmary
rest periods
sleeping bags
deepwater test
counselors bringing back pizza in the middle of the night
short sheeting
poison ivy
calamine lotion
bug juice
screen doors
taps

BATTLING TOPS

CHEERIO YO-YOS

CHINESE JUMP ROPES

EDMOND'S SCIENTIFIC

LINCOLN LOGS

MAD LIBS

SILLY STRING

TINKERTOYS

CREEPY CRAWLERS

Wonder Bread

Underwood Deviled Ham

Spam

Sloppy Joes

Shake 'N Bake

Hamburger Helper

Aerosol cheese

Rice-A-Roni

Vienna sausages

tuna casserole

pigs in a blanket

Eggo waffles

Cup-A-Soup

Instant mashed potatoes

Campbell's Soup

Tang

Hunt's Snack Pack
Rice Krispies treats
Reggie Bars
Dilly Bars
Devil Dogs
The Marathon Bar
Fudgsicles
Crazy Straws
Big Buddy Bubble Gum
candy necklaces
Jolly Ranchers
Jujubes
Now and Laters
Mr. Softee Ice Cream
all-day suckers
Ring Pops

Scooter Pies
Good Humor ice cream man
Fudge Town Cookies
Count Chocula and Franken Berry
Pudding Pops
Ring Dings
pink marshmallow Snoballs
Twinkies
Abba-Zabas
Zotz
jawbreakers
Good & Plenty
Fireballs
Pixy Stix
Candy Dots
SweeTarts

QUAKER
QUISP

Yogi Bear & Booboo

Kimba the White Lion

H. R. Pufnstuf

Speed Racer

Grape Ape

New Zoo Review

The Archies

In the News

Johnny Quest

Top Cat

Scooby-Doo

Magilla Gorilla

Secret Squirrel
& Morocco Mole

Fractured
Fairytales

Wonderama

Speed Buggy

Sherman & Mr. Peabody

Dudley-do-right

Space Ghost

Underdog

The Banana Splits

Shazam and Isis

Wacky Races

Tennessee Tuxedo

The Jetsons

Penelope Pitstop

Granny & Precious

Fat Albert & the Cosby Kids

Schoolhouse Rock

TOSS

Metal toys

Go Fish!

Hot Wheels

"You sunk my battleship."

flipping baseball cards

toy Texaco trucks

A C R O S S

wooden blocks

Creepy Crawlers

Hess trucks

Uno

Ouija boards

aggies and puries

here come de judge
Flying Fickle Finger of Fate Award
sock it to me
One Ringy Dingy,
Two Ringy Dingies
very interesting, but stupid

"I can name that tune in **four** notes."

"I can name that tune in **three** notes."

"I can name that tune in **two** notes."

"Marjorie, **Name That Tune.**"

Crying Indian litter commercial

Actually getting up to change the channel

"Makeup!" giant powder puff

Kitty Carlisle on "What's My Line?"

Black-and-white TV sets

Cigarette advertisements

"Carol, show us what's behind Door Number 3."

American-made televisions

"Beam me up, Scotty."

Late-night TV before infomercials

"Send it to Zoom, Box 350, Boston, MA 02134"

When TV channels went off the air at night

?

a- Life cereal. b- Calgon. c- Imperial Margarine. d- Wendy's Restaurant.
e- Alka Seltzer. f- Ken-L-Ration. g- Razzles. h- Kellogg's Frosted Flakes.

a

b

c

d

e

f

g

h

"HEY MIKEY, HE LIKES IT!"

"Ancient Chinese Secret, huh?"

"It's not nice to fool Mother Nature."

"WHERE'S THE BEEF?"

"I can't believe I ate the whole thing!"

"My dog is better than your dog."

"Is it a candy, or is it a gum?"

"They're Gr-r-reat!"

“It’s a floor wax, it’s a dessert topping.”

“Puppy Uppers and Doggie Downers”

Live

Babwa-Wawa

Samurai Delicatessen

Garrett Morris as Idi “VD” Amin

Emily Litella

Bad Theatre with Leonard Pinth-Garnell

New Yo

“We are from France.”

“Schwing!”

Saturda

“I’m Chevy Chase and you’re not.”

Mr. Mike Meets Uncle Remus

“Vito, you’re blocking.”

Bill Murray as a lounge singer

Jake and Elwood Blues

Bass-O-Matic

Gimme Mick!

The Judy Miller Show

"We want your pollen."

"It's always something."

from

"Jane, you ignorant slut!"

"Ooooh Noooooooo. . ."

Chevy Chase falling down

Don Pardo

rk, it's

"No Coke, Pepsi."

"I am Gumby, dammit!"

y Night!

Placenta Helper

The Widends

special prom noogies

"Land Shark"

The Not Ready For Prime Time Players

"We are two wild and crazy guys."

E. Buzz Miller's Animal Kingdom

PAN AM

North Central
Republic
Airport '75
before frequent flyer miles
Eastern
pianos on 747s
Braniff
People Express
Freddy Laker and the Skytrain
chiclets gum
the air-traffic controllers strike
before business class
crossing the tarmac and going up stairs to get on the plane
Idlewild Airport
smoking on domestic flights
New York Air
Capitol Air
The Trump Shuttle
painful headphones
metal "wings" pin
propeller planes
The Concorde

1. I have a dream that one day on the hills of Georgia the sons of former slaves and the sons of former slaveowners will be able to sit down together at the table of brotherhood.
2. That's one small step for [a] man, one giant leap for mankind.
3. In the future everyone will be world-famous for fifteen minutes.
4. We are not fighting for integration, nor are we fighting for separation. We are fighting for recognition as human beings. We are fighting for . . . human rights.
5. Power is the great aphrodisiac.
6. And so, my fellow Americans, ask not what your country can do for you; ask what you can do for your country.
7. You don't need a weatherman to know which way the wind blows.
8. When an individual is taken into custody or otherwise deprived of his freedom by the authorities and is subjected to questioning . . . he must be warned prior to any questioning that he has the right to remain silent, that anything he says can be used against him in a court of law, that he has the right to the presence of an attorney, and that if he cannot afford an attorney one will be appointed for him prior to any questioning if he so desires.
9. Nice guys finish last.
10. We know what a person thinks not when he tells us what he thinks, but by his actions.

1.H 2.J 3.G 4.B 5.F 6.E 7.C 8.D 9.I 10.A

A. Isaac Bashevis Singer
B. Malcolm X
C. Bob Dylan
D. Earl Warren
E. John Fitzgerald Kennedy
F. Henry Kissinger
G. Andy Warhol
H. Dr. Martin Luther King, Jr.
I. Leo Durocher
J. Neil Armstrong

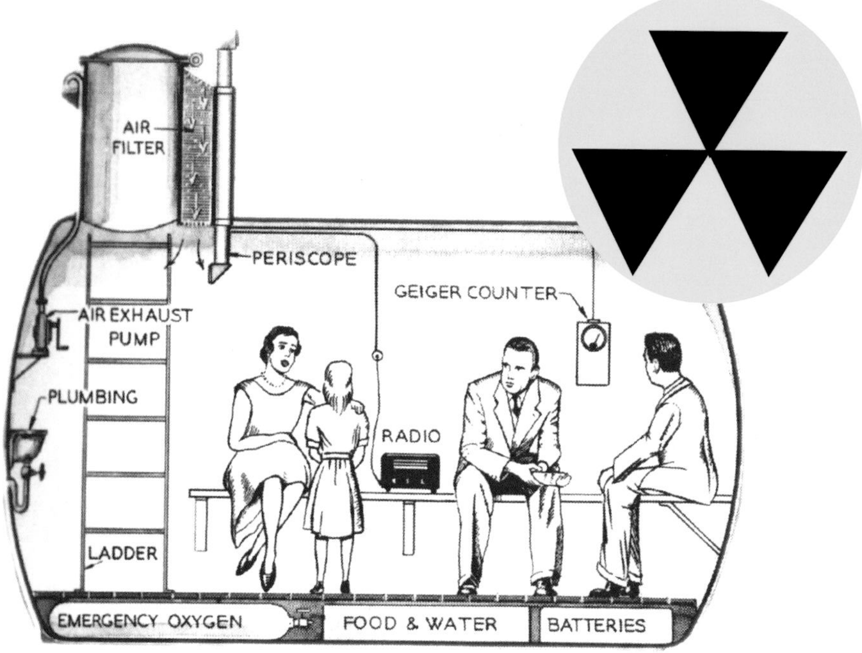

apartheid *Vietnam*
neutron bomb The Falklands
cuba before castro
Grenada SPUTNIK
korean war Solidarity
drop/cover drill

NMARK
U.S.S.R
EAST GERMANY
POLAND
GERMANY
CZECHOSLOVAKIA
AUSTRIA
HUNGARY
ROMANIA
YUGOSLAVIA
ITALY
BULGARIA
ALB.
T
TURKEY
GREECE

tell fortunes
with
magic
"8 BALL"®
FORTUNE
TELLER
8
®

crazy 8's

8 track tapes

8 millimeter home movies

8 Is Enough

"Sit on it!"

To Tell the Truth Room 222

Gunsmoke Maude

The Flying Nun

Potsie F Troop

Tonto The Courtship of Eddie's Father

Julia Art Linkletter

The Mod Squad Uncle Miltie

That Girl Quincy

The Loretta Young Show

Rat Patrol

Donna Reed Mission Impossible

The Fonz "Daniel Boone was a man, was a big man. . ."

Dark Shadows Bonanza

KRAFTWERK
Talk Talk
Debbie Gibson
The Lords Of The New Church
OXO
Heaven 17
Dead Or Alive
Kajagoogoo
TOM TOM CLUB

Yello

Alphaville
Haircut One Hundred
The Art of Noize
Ebn-Ozn
Men Without Hats
Thrashing Doves

BLONDIE

a-ha

A Flock of Seagulls
The The
Split Enz
Bow Wow Wow
Kim Carnes
Quarterflash
Icicle Works
Dexy's Midnight Runners
Hipsway
The Outfield

HAVE A NICE DAY!

l

m

n

Didn't find *your* fondest memory in **Do You Remember?** Phone, or fax it, to us for Volume Two at (212) 873-7223. Or, e-mail us your suggestions. Reach us on-line at TakeUBack@aol.com or on the Web at http://www.doyouremember.com